Ruth
May beautiful things happen in your life in 1999.
Harry Knitter 4/99

A Sweet Sampling
of Floral Delights

by harry knitter

Uncle Buck's Restaurant
Easter Sunday 4/4/99

A Sweet Sampling
of Floral Delights

For anyone who enjoys

getting, giving or gazing

at flowers.

Kordene Publications, Ltd.

Okemos, Michigan, U.S.A

Published by Kordene Publications, Ltd.
4463 Copperhill, Okemos, Michigan 48864, USA

Publisher's Cataloging-in-Publication Data

A Sweet Sampling of Floral Delights /for anyone who enjoys getting, giving, or gazing at flowers / by Harry Knitter, Okemos, Michigan; Kordene Publications, 1998.
p. cm. (Potpourri series)
Includes bibliographical references. ISBN 0-9652333-2-4
1. Flowers – Literary collections. 2.Humor 3.Poetry

Printed in the United States of America

Table of Contents

Table of Contents (cont.)

Acknowledgements

I would like to thank the following individuals for their valuable contributions to this book:

To my wife, Nancy, for providing superb feedback–most of which I followed.

To Shelee Bush, for getting excited about this project, doing an outstanding job on the art and layout, and for keeping me on my game.

To Tom Gennara, for an excellent front cover photo.

To Jim Jordan and Bill Golden of FTD, for saying "yes".

To Fran Johnson, for her first-rate advice.

To the Jenkins Group, especially Theresa Nelson and Alex Moore, for hanging in when the going got rough.

To Debbie Wilcox-Jamieson, for her constant encouragement.

To Linda Peckham, for starting me on my way.

I am particularly indebted to the FTD Association for generously allowing me to reprint some of the florist stories originally published in FTD Family magazine. Their support is sincerely appreciated.

About the Author...

Harry Knitter loves to view, hold, draw, photograph, and talk about flowers. He also writes about flowers in floral trade magazines, in advertising copy, in correspondence, and in poems dedicated to his wife, Nancy. He loves flowers and other people who love flowers.

He once was the marketing director of the world's largest floral organization, FTD, and introduced the successful FTD Pick-Me-Up® Bouquet.

He enjoys being surrounded with flowers and with beautiful depictions of flowers.

He feels that beauty is contagious. So far it hasn't worked on him.

Dedications

To my wife, Nancy,
who inspires me to
write about the beautiful
dimensions of living

To my mother, Eleanor,
who has found peace
and abundant joy

To Janet Culver,
who will always be
in our hearts.
She taught us to treasure
each moment of life

Preface

I wrote this book because I wanted to express my love for flowers and for things beautiful.

It has no plot, no real theme, and no underlying esoteric message. It is a "sampling,"as suggested in the title. Therefore, you can taste the poetry, savor the prose, relish the stories, and smile or cry as you react to the content of each page. In fact, I hope you'll read your favorite parts many times over.

It doesn't matter whether you begin at the beginning or jump in at the 2/3 point. It's a potpourri, remember, and I want it to be what you want it to be.

And most of all, I want it to do justice to one of God's finest creations.

Can you smell the roses?

– harry knitter, author

Introduction

Life is beautiful...

And flowers are an important part of life.

From the beginning of time,

flowers have helped us to communicate with each other

...and sometimes with ourselves.

We have sent them to the young mother to celebrate new life;

And we have sent them to express our sympathy

and our sorrow to the bereaved.

We have presented them to those we love

And we have delivered them to cheer the ill.

And we have sometimes bought them for no particular reason, because we enjoy being surrounded by beauty and color and delicate grace.

We have painted them, written about them in song, in poetry, and in prose. Flowers are among the Lord's finest creations. Enjoy the fruits of His labors. Make flowers a beautiful part of your day every day.

Flowers from **A**

Alive Beautiful Communicative

Delicate *Elegant* Festive *Fragrant*

Fun GRAND *Glorious* *Gorgeous*

Habit-Forming Inimitable Joyous

K*ind-hearted* Lovely MAGNIFICENT

Natural *Opulent* Pretty

Quintessential Romanti

Sentimental

Terrific Underappreciated

Versatile WONDERFUL

eXotic Young-at-Heart

ZANY

to Z

1 THE MAGIC OF A SINGLE ROSE

Nobody knows

How just one solitary rose

Can start or enhance

A budding romance

Is it the smell?

Not one of us can tell;

But something causes the tingle

That keeps us from staying single.

You'd expect the prickly thorn

to prevent romance from being born.

But when the wedding vows are repeated,

Can't we logically assume

It is the Rose that causes lasting love to bloom?

When two become one.

Thoughts of Springtime

We are never really quite the same after love ignites a life-long flame
And tulips touch ever so gently...
Days go by and we go on living; and soon we find ourselves forgiving
And tulips touch ever so silently...
Love comes our way in daily ration, expressed with happiness and passion
And tulips touch ever so warmly...
I felt so sad, and often lonely; then you became my one and only
When tulips touch ever so reassuringly...
The love we give, the words we say will never leave, or drift away
When tulips touch ever so faithfully.
Our love will grow endlessly.

Get Well

The aches, the pains;

first the clouds hide the sun. . .

and then it rains.

Every hour without a flower

is like a big, black cloud

and a thunder shower.

The room is dark

and there's no spark.

Nothing but stillness

and days full of pillness.

Then recuperative powers

Come alive with flowers:

Red! Orange! and Yellow!

"We're Here!," they bellow!

Wake up and perk up. . .

There are projects to work up!

Good health is a blessing;

"Protect it," we're constantly stressing.

But if you are sick and in pain this hour

Look to the magical healing power

Of a lovely, delicate, fragrant fresh flower.

Get well.

The Bridal Bouquet

How can an event

so happy,

so festive,

so fresh as a day in May

Be associated with a bouquet

that's called a

"Nosegay?"

Should it be sprayed

with antihistamine?

And after all the work that is devoted

to the design and creation of wedding bouquets,

How could we allow them to

be hurled through the air

like a frisbee?

or a boomerang?

or a bag of peanuts?

or a six pack of micro brew?

into the waiting hands of the happy bride-to-be.

Who will, in time, repeat the same

process. . .

as if it were

the right thing to do. Boo.

Flowers for a Little Girl

Her life is full of turmoil and noise—a total, complete, and unadulterated whirl.
That's our Kayla, our granddaughter, our blossom with ponytails, our favorite girl.
When she plays the piano, her little feet dangle
To us, she's beautiful from any angle.
She strokes each key with ladylike grace
But don't miss the mischief behind her smiling face.
She plays the simplest form of song –"Twinkle, Twinkle"...care to sing along?
And she gets excited and chatters for hours, when her loving grandad sends her flowers.
She likes the colors, shows them to her friends
and talks about her gift until each busy day ends.
Her grandpa beams as he savors the mysterious powers
of Kayla's wonderful gift of fragrant flowers
And so, dear florist, please send a lovely bouquet
to the little girl who dangled her feet when she played our piano.
One key at a time. One enchanting day.

A florist in Arizona

was working with a nervous young man who predicted that he'd forget

what to ask for when he returned to pick up his flowers the following week.

"It's called a Nosegay," the florist repeated.

"Think of the beautiful fragrance you enjoy with your ***nose****."*

"NOSEGAY."

The young man returned a week later and had prepared himself mentally

to remember what to ask for.

Still he was nervous.

With a deep breath and an extra dose of courage, he approached the counter and said.

"I came to pick up some flowers for my nostrils."

The Game of ~~NAMES~~ ~~names~~

n - a - m - e - s

I can't say it's exactly fun and games to remember a list of flower names.

(No matter what anyone claims)

Who hasn't suffered a sudden case of amnesia

when they try to recall the fantastic, fancy freesia?

As for me, I'd rather face a case of diptheria

Than to be asked to think of the name for alstroemeria.

I'm a typical man, you see, and flower names are forgettable

That they don't call them Bears, Bruisers and Packers is regrettable.

And if a rose by any other name is still a rose,

As William claims, I guess we'll just have to rely on our nose.

Loveliness in Aisle Six

Among the rusting carts and candy hearts
is an oasis of delight:

Supermarket flowers

There's no ambiance
or semblance
of romance.
Just buckets of blooms
One logically assumes
Will generate smiles when sadness looms.

And oh! Soft and squeezable Teddy Bears
Leaning up against the prickly pears

There for our thoughtful consideration
(Have him hold a single carnation).
When you present him as a gift.
(While you're here,
may as well pick up a fifth.)
And over by the beans
some nice fresh leafy greens
To fill in the gaps
Before the counter boy wraps
Our delicate floral treats
(Yesterday, by the way, he wrapped red meats).

The Random Thoughts

I've planned and organized a thousand details
And pray that all's well that goes well.
There's no turning back, no stopping the express
Unless the whole plan goes berserk; but who can tell?
I wonder if his mom's new dress
Will arrive in time to dazzle and impress.
And will his dad's rental tux fit OK?
He hasn't worn a tie since his graduation day.
Is the red-haired flower girl all prepared and ready
to be calm, cute, cool, and steady?
And could my love, the groom, be having reservations
About commitment or singular preservation?

# of an 11th-Hour Bride

There's so much to think about
Through all my hectic waking hours.
Thank the Lord for moments of peace and fulfillment
That accompany the beauty of flowers. What powers!
When they arrived at my door, by surprise,
I was so overwhelmed with joy I cried.
(Tomorrow, when the celebration is over,
I'll be so happy the knot is finally tied)..
The beauty of flowers will always cheer us
And we'll want them in our home, so near us.
As we begin our life together, we'll always treasure
The love we share, and the values only we can measure

Any Chance There Are Ants in Your Plants?

It seems to me

That there will never be

Anything quite so fancy free

As the soothing power

of a freshly cut flower.

And yet...

another of God's creations

Deserves to share in life's plot:

Displayed in a terra cotta pot

With green leaves and stunning blooms

Plants brighten our dreary, colorless rooms.

PSSSSSSssssssssSSSST!

Mums in the fall
Azaleas for yuletide spirit
Tulips in the spring.
Next to a bouquet,
they're a perfect way
To color our day.
And we'd look silly
Should we forget the lily.
Trumpeting the Easter prayer
And reminding us He was there.
If, by chance
Our lovely, leafy plants
Became infested with pesky ants
There's only one thing to say: Let us spray.

Ants?......

No
Chance.

Bon Voyage *Sister Dearest:*

So you're sailing off to faraway places,

To see white sands, green water, and sunburnt faces.

You're lucky to get all that money from rich aunt Sophie

Who always considered you to be the family trophy.

As for me, I'm stuck here in my hairdressing job

And my husband Frank is still a lazy, no-good slob

But forget all that, let's bury the hatchet

(If something bad happens, I'm likely to catch it.)

Aunt Sophie's gone and in the casket

So Frank and me sent you this fruit basket

Have fun, dear sister, and Bon Voyage

I'm busy selling old dresses in our broken down garage,

Be sure to send postcards.

Love,
Your Sister

Flowers & Funerals

Flowers from the earliest times may have been placed on the bodies of the dead for sentimental as well as practical purposes (the fragrance of flowers was needed because there was no embalming). In terms of symbolism, flowers represented beauty that had a mortality to it.[1]

It's true that flowers bring beauty to our lives in many different ways.

And the presence of flowers helps us to mark the most significant occasions of our lives, from birth through death.

But flowers have finite lifespans, as all of us do.

Take good care of that flower; give it tender love and care, and it will bring joy to you.

And do the same for those you hold dear.

[1] *the Wonderful World of Superstitions, Prophesy and Love, by Leonard Ashley.*

In Lieu of Flowers

It's like whispering

"In lieu of respect for the deceased"

"In lieu of fond memories"

"In lieu of fragrance"

"In lieu of sentiment"

"In lieu of happiness"

"In lieu of beauty"

"In lieu of comfort"

"In lieu of color"

"In lieu of life"

In lieu of you

As experienced by an Ohio florist,

"Please Omit Flowers" is a big problem for retail florists.

And sometimes, the reason for the Please Omit is not a routine response.

For example:

"Our delivery man, Roger, returned to the flower shop after taking several deliveries to a local funeral home. He told us that the funeral home was not allowing any flowers to be placed in the room with the body of the deceased."

The reason?

"Uncle Leo is allergic to flowers," the groomsman reported dutifully.

Consequently, the family had ordered a plastic casket spray of silk flowers, thinking that fresh blooms might somehow get their uncle out of sorts due to his allergy.

Uncle Leo would have been proud of their effort to protect him from discomfort.

In New Jersey,

as in most other states, future brides who meet with their florist to select wedding flowers are unfamiliar with all of the choices they have to make and the decisions don't often come without reservations.

The florist went on to say,

"I was consulting with a very excited future bride about her flowers. Little by little, the young woman proceeded to pick out all of the flowers she wanted in the church, at the reception, and at the rehearsal dinner." Going one step farther, the florist asked the bride whether an aisle runner should be provided for the wedding. Somewhat rattled by the unexpected question, the nervous young lady said,

"No–no runner is needed. We have ushers."

The florist realized, at that moment, that the bride-to-be pictured someone in a track outfit dashing off the deliver important messages about the wedding to unidentified recipients. The wedding went on without an aisle runner.

Modern Day Convenience:
THE TOLL-FREE NUMBER

I think that I will never see

The florist I order from toll-free

She's out there, somewhere, some place,

But will I ever see her smiling face?

I listen to her voice

So pleasant, so warm and so nice.

But a face-to-face encounter can never be

Because, you see, she comes to me toll-free.

When she speaks

My attention peaks.

My composure becomes like soft, slippery, gushy lard.

Especially when she whispers softly,

"Will You be Using Your Credit Card?"

Though she knows

Where my order goes

She'll never find out

What I'm all about. For. . .

I think that I shall never see

the florist who takes my order toll-free.

Wallflowers

Wallflowers (sob) don't get invited to the dance (cue the tears)

And rarely even have half a chance at romance.

They sit by themselves, gazing vacantly into open space

with a plain, mundane, arcane look on their face.

No one ever knows that they're even around

So they hardly ever, ever hardly make a solitary sound.

Wallflowers think of life as an empty glass

And each day brings still another big old morass.

But some wallflowers soak up rays

from the sun and decide to be

more than expected by anyone.

they bloom and develop, and force

themselves to smile; without warn-

ing, they are suddenly able to charm

and beguile. Their lives are transformed

into tales like Hansel and Gretel.

And soon they're putting their dainty little petals

to the metal. They're out in the crowd, on the beach,

in the mall And now they have become like you and me–

(though a bit off the wall).

The Day the Bear Died

One of the most valuable employees in the floral industry over the past 30 years was "Dr. Death", Bud Lipinski. He got his nickname by being ubiquitous in the funeral and sympathy sector of the flower market and through his untiring efforts to have flowers portrayed positively whenever a celebrity or notable person passed away. Bud would jump on a plane and jet off to some far-off spot almost every week to work with local florists who were designing arrangements for funerals of dignitaries.

One afternoon, Bud was in his office when the phone rang. He picked it up and heard a tearful lady florist on the other end of the line who was obviously in great distress.

"Bud," she announced, "the Bear died!"

Bud was mystified. "Why, dear lady, would you call me because some dumb bear died?"

It was a crank call, he decided.

"No, Bud, I'm calling from Alabama, and the Bear is Paul "Bear" Bryant, long-time coach of the Alabama football team.

" 'The Bear' is one of the heroes of our state, and his widow has asked me to design a casket blanket in red and crimson carnations, with the Alabama Crimson Tide logo on it. I don't know how to do it, Bud, can you help me?"

So she was serious, he concluded.

Then he began to describe the process of weaving the stems of carnations through burlap and fastening a backing material that would protect the surface of the casket. When he finished, she was ready to design the blanket.

A day later, the floral blanket in crimson and white was on every television set in the country as the "Bear's" funeral was afforded national coverage because of his extraordinary record as a coach and as a man.

10,000 carnations were used to make up the display.

And Dr. Death had come through once again.

A New England Florist

thought her new salesperson had adapted well to her new job.

In her first two weeks in the shop, the woman seemed

willing to learn and had made no serious mistakes.

Then a grieving family came in the front door and told the sales clerk

they had come to the shop to order a casket spray.

"Oh, you don't have to order it," the inexperienced salesperson said.

"I'm sure I should be able to find an aerosol can of it in the backroom somewhere."

Songs With Floral Roots

I'm Sending You a Big Bouquet of Roses
(One for Every Time You Broke My Heart)

Sweet Violets

You Don't Bring Me Flowers Any More

Lily Marlene

Tiptoe Through the Tulips

Daisy, Daisy

I'll Be With You in Apple Blossom Time

Sweet Violets

Cherry Pink and Apple Blossom White

When You Wore a Tulip (And I Wore a Big Red Rose)

Days of Wine and Roses

Room Full of Roses

I'm Sending You a Big Bouquet of Roses

Red Roses for a Blue Lady

Roses of Picardy

Rose Room

Moonlight and Roses

Honeysuckle Rose

La Vie En Rose

(Give Me) One Dozen Roses

Rose of Washington Square

Second-Hand Rose

The Wisconsin florist

arrived at the address of the person

who was to receive a gorgeous bouquet of peach-colored roses.

A little boy, about 11 years old with a freckled face and toothless grin,

sat on the steps of the house.

"Is your mother at home?," the delivery person asked.

"Yep," said the boy.

So the florist climbed the stairs and rang the doorbell.

And rang again. And rang again.

No one responded.

"I thought you said your mother is at home," the frustrated florist declared.

"She is," the boy repeated, "I live next door."

Not a Reason Needed, *Nor a Season Needed*

If you're looking for a reason

Or waiting for that certain season

To project an image that's a cut above

when you send flowers to the one you love.

Flowers can lift someone's spirits today,

Make them as happy as a child at play.

Put some petals on their dinner table,

Just as many as you're fiscally able.

Remember it's the thought and not the price

That makes your floral gift so wonderfully nice.

When you surprise someone for no reason at all

You'll be remembered in summer, spring, winter, and fall.

A Bouquet for Granny

Who has ever heard any discouraging word

from a Grandmother?

It seems almost uncanny

That <u>everyone's</u> favorite granny likes flowers . . .

when they come from redhead Danny,

Stephanie, Bobby and curly-topped Annie.

So the way to Granny's loving heart is to give her flowers

(now that's downright smart!)

So listen, kids, send her a gorgeous bouquet

And live to love her smile for the entire day.

In California,

a florist was complaining that her legs ached because of the trips she had to make up and down the stairs to the store's second level, where the Mercury computer printer was located. During a week preceding the holiday, the florist and her Yorkshire terrier, Freeway, ran up the stairs to pick up order printouts as many as 30 times each day.

Then she hatched a brilliant idea.

On her next trip upstairs, she tied the order printouts to Freeway's collar and asked the designers downstairs to call him. In a flash, Freeway had bounded down the steps and delivered the orders to one of the members of the design team.

Upstairs, the florist wiped her brow and laughed. It turned out that the solution to her problem had been right under her nose all along.

Dear Secretary:

Roses are red,

Violets are blue.

If I give you roses

Stella will want me to take her

on a cruise to Peru.

So. . .

Gettin' Ready for the Senior Prom

I didn't think I had the slightest chance

When I asked sweet Leslie to the dance.

But she agreed to be my date

And the night is guaranteed to be great.

Her "yes" was this man's perfect dream

(Better not run out of acne cream).

But now I've got so much to do

And I-I-I-m nervvvous —weren't you?

Buy the tickets, rent a tux, wash the car

That's not the total list, by far.

I'm running out of days and hours

Think I'll run out and order flowers.

So Mr. Florist, make the choices easy for me

For I've never done this before, you see.

A cool corsage is what I'm after

(Hope she doesn't break into hysterical laughter).

Her dress is blue like her pretty eyes

And I'll be the envy of all the guys

If you make me a hero I'll be back

Do I pin them on or use a thumb tack?

There's no tellin' how we'll do

But I'm going' to dance

with the girl in blue.

A Florist in North Carolina

took an order over the phone from a nice lady

who wanted to send flowers for the funeral

of her dear old aunt Betty.

She discussed at length the type of bouquet she wanted

to have delivered to the funeral home, the where and the when.

Finally, she said she wanted to charge the purchase on her credit card.

She gave the florist her VISA card number.

Then, when asked for the expiration date, she turned to her husband and said,

"Honey, on what day did Betty die?"

Ode to a Mother-in-Law

Your daughter loves you so very much and though distance separates us from you

She tries to frequently keep in touch through snow and sleet and occasional flu.

She married me for better or for worse (Didn't realize "worse" meant corny verse)

We've traveled the world, and I'm always proud

Of her style and grace–she stands out in a crowd.

You've brought her up in the very best way

To follow your path, and may I say I'm not sure exactly what she saw

In me, but I'm sure glad she takes after you,

Dear Mother-in-Law.

The Delivery Man

You probably don't remember me

But I'm the truck-drivin' guy

Who delivers flowers to your door

and hears you say, "Now who are these for?"

You respond ever so quickly

When I ring your front door bell.

You always look surprised

And obviously excited as well.

I drive around the city all day

Making people happy when I say

"Dear Lady, these flowers are for you,"

Then stand back as their smile comes through..

I don't make much money,

Put on thousands of miles

Exist on minimum wages

But sure beats cleanin' cages.

Someday, I hope that someone

Will think enough of me

To send me a bouquet that's sweet

For the friendly delivery man–Pete.

A New York Florist

experienced the unspoiled, spontaneous humor of kids when the driver delivered an "It's a Girl!" arrangement to a suburban home. As he pulled up in front of the house, he noticed a preschooler playing in the yard.

The little boy came up to the fence and asked, "Who are you?"

The driver, in a joke-around mood, repeated the question: "Who are *<u>you?"</u>*

"I'm nobody," the boy responded.

"Aw, come on," the driver continued, "I'll bet you're somebody.

In fact, I''ll bet your name is Smith."

The boy was intrigued. "How did you know that?"

"I know everything," the driver said. I know that you're a cute little boy

and that you have a new baby sister.

And I know that your baby sister just came home from the hospital

and her name is Mary."

(he had read the enclosure card accompanying the bouquet.)

The tyke was dazzled.

He looked the driver straight in the eyes and said, "Are you GOD?"

The driver was touched. "No," he said,

"I'm not God, but I know that God loves little boys like you

and that these flowers will make your mom smile."

Together they walked to the front door and rang the doorbell.

When someone sends *flowers* to a MAN

I like to grunt and crush aluminum cans

And wouldn't be seen with also-rans.

I'm a macho man, and don't you forget it,

With a crazy old hound that drools when you pet it.

I fish and hunt and drink beer with the best.

(My tattoo says, "In God I Trust, But Forget the Rest").

Most nights, you'll find me out with the boys

Playing pool or racing one of my motorized toys.

Now come over here and let me whisper in your ear. I confess

that I like to get flowers and here's my address.

I'm not a sissy because I love things of beauty— my girl, she likes roses (Her name is Trudy).

She sent some red ones with green leafy stuff

If you don't like the idea, I have to say: "TOUGH!"

I'm no sissy and if you should wonder, I'll kick your a__ and boot you over yonder.

If you ask me, there's nothing wrong in your plan when you decide to send colorful blooms to your man.

He may drop what he's doing and dial up the phone

So you won't have to spend the evening alone.

Turn off the tube, pick up bell's invention and make me your exclusive center of attention.

I love women, flowers and cold Bud Light

If you don't like it, get ready to fight.

In Pennsylvania,

a florist witnessed the perfect solution to a common problem involving a child. The little flower girl was crying and screaming and categorically refused to go down the aisle of the church. As if that was not enough of a problem, she had crawled under the piano in the choir room and would not come out despite the wedding party's best efforts.

The florist elected to take control of the situation by proposing a challenge to the little girl. She reported that she took all of the pennies out of her change purse, making sure that the obstinate girl saw everything the florist was doing. Then she spread the pennies between the flowers in the little girl's woven carrier.

"I told her that she could have all the pennies for her very own after she came back up the aisle," he reported. With visions of pennies dancing in her head, the girl responded beautifully.

"Not only did she go down the aisle smiling at everybody, charming all of the people in the congregation, but she held the basket with the greatest of care and caution, watching it as she walked down the aisle to make sure she had not spilled some of the flowers onto the runner."

No flowers dropped. No pennies dropped either.

During a brief reception following the wedding the florist learned that the winning idea and her decisive action was the talk of the reception. Within a few minutes after her arrival, she was cornered by two of the guests and wound up being asked to submit bids on two new wedding projects for the following month.

Originality makes solutions out of problems every day.

And that's what creativity is all about

Can flowers talk?

The ways in which you use flowers

in your home

will send

messages

to your guests.

For example:

Flowers near your front door tell guests that you perceive their visit as somthing special, out of the ordinary.

Flowers like eucalyptus of hydrangea on a mantel provide a bridge between architecture and floral design.

Floral centerpieces say "We're glad you came" to dinner guests. The most popular flowers for centerpieces are roses, carnations, mums, pompons, daisies, and sunflowers.

With overnight guests, flowers in the bedroom indicate that you're delighted they are staying with you. A plant makes a welcome statement as well.

Fun with Fantasy Flowers

Have You Ever Seen a DandyLion?

The Question

That Floral Delivery People

Hear Many Times

Every Day:

"These Flowers Are for **Me?**"

A Carolina florist

tells the story of an experienced delivery person being sent to a local area town to drop off a bud vase and panda bear. A routine delivery? Wrong. Even though the lights were on at the house, there was no response to the doorbell, so the driver went around the back of the house to see if she could find someone from the family of the recipient. That's where she encountered the lonely billy goat. "He took an immediate liking to her, the flowers, and the Honda wagon she was driving," the florist reported. After climbing from the car hood onto the roof, the goat proceeded to slide down the front windshield and pester the florist for attention..

She finally managed to get out of the car when the goat wandered off temporarily. The delivery woman placed the bud vase on a high window sill and left.

When she returned to the floral shop, the delivery woman called the recipient to advise her about the location of the flowers.

"Oh, we found them," the woman announced.

"And so did our goat, who enjoyed a nice snack of roses and daisies."

The florist agreed meekly to replace the flowers and the bear.

From that point on, the delivery person's nick name became **"Billy"** *for obvious reasons.*

If *Flowers* Were Other Sweet Things...

What's your favorite flower for *Sweetest Day?*

The elegant rose would be a rich chocolate covered cherry, the favorite choice of everyone.

The carnation would be a freshly-dipped scoop of strawberry ice cream on a crispy cone.

The poppy would be a hot 'n' spicy candy—with a peppery, zesty flavor and a pungent fragrance.

The gerbera daisy would be a giant lollipop with bright colors and a long stem to keep your fingers from getting sticky.

A florist on Long Island

hired a new "gopher"—

a high school youngster who needed part-time work.

His first assignment was to run an errand to the supermarket

to pick up a supply of fruit for some fruit basket arrangements.

He was gone about an hour

And finally returned

With a bag that contained

a watermelon

and two lemons.

Petaling our way home

I hope you enjoyed your brief interlude

With flowers that create a positive attitude.

If, however, your thinking is still in disarray,

Buy one rose–and then a full bouquet.

It doesn't matter if you don't know their names

If you want to, call them Jason, Michael and James.

Just keep flowers around you all day long,

And when you're at home, hum a flower song.

Stay on the path you enjoy the most

And when you meet the goal set for yourself

Put on something extra special, something nice

And put a liter of champagne on ice.

Toast your success and flash a friendly smile

You're feelin' better than you have for awhile.

Now you're prepared to face any test

With a positive outlook that's truly the best.

Treat yourself to some pretty petals today

Flower Buying Tips

To get the most value when you're buying flowers, try these suggestions:

• Always order before the busiest times, just prior to a holiday like Christmas or Mother's Day. If you place your order during the peak demand period, be prepared to pay more and get less service than at other times when the pace is less hectic.

• Give the designer some options. Don't design the bouquet yourself; leave the creative process to the designers, give them some leeway in stretching their creative muscles, and you'll be pleased with the results. And be sure to express your appreciation of their talents.

• Become a regular customer. When you order from the same florist they'll get to know your likes and dislikes and try to keep you coming back for more.

• Don't be afraid to take in your own container to be filled with flowers. Florists like to sell flowers, not baskets.

• Occasionally, ask them to create something out of the ordinary. They'll work extra hard to give you a bouquet that will stir your senses.

• Tell them where your arrangement will be located, so they can make it just right for the setting.

Caring for your

Your florist wants you to experience the beauty of flowers for as long as possible. To prolong the enjoyment of your floral delights, try these tips:

• Always ask the florist about the freshness of the flowers you're purchasing. If they have been in the cooler for several days, try another variety that may have just arrived.

• Ask for a packet of preservative.

(note: don't use powder preservative with bulb flowers like tulips).

• Place flower stems under water and cut off about one inch from the bottom. Try to make your cut on an angle so more water will be absorbed up the stem.

flowers

- Immerse stems in lukewarm water mixed with preservative.
- Keep flowers out of direct sunlight or heat flow.

  Also do not expose flowers to freezing temperatures.
- Remove dead leaves and foliage.
- Water daily. Add more preservative.
- Clean and sanitize vase after using.

Sending Flowers Around the World

When the flowers-by-wire service was first established in 1910, it became possible to place an order for a specified arrangement in one city and have it delivered in another city...or in a far-off corner of the world, as the system eventually expanded. The main ingredients of this service were: a means of communication between the sending and delivering florist; a directory of florists on the system; the presence of a selection guide in each florist's shop, and; a clearinghouse to process the transaction, ensuring that both florists were paid their fair share of the total amount remitted by the customer.

For many years, order information was transmitted via telegraph; then, the telephone and telex; in the '70's, the computer took over, since aided by fax machines and toll-free telephone lines. The latter methods threaten the very existence of the wire services in the future, because consumers can now communicate directly with the delivering florist and place their orders without involving a florist in their own locale. The delivering florist can provide a catalog of arrangements to the customer by direct mail... or on a web page over the Internet. Direct ordering by the consumer via the computer is the latest step in the sophistication of a system that began 85 years ago as a simple teletype message from one florist to another:

Say It with Flowers.

Communica

For a long time, the telephone served as the primary means of communicating floral orders from one florist to another. As sales volumes grew at holiday times, however, it became increasingly difficult for many florists to reach their counterparts in other sections of the U.S. and Canada on certain peak traffic days; for example, the days of the week preceding Mother's Day and Christmas, when millions of flower-buyers were trying to send bouquets and plants to friends or loved ones across the continent, spanning different time zones.

In the late '70's, the same man who eventually developed Airphone® on jet liners came up with the concept of Mercury®, a computerized communications link between florists throughout North America. With Mercury, orders for flowers could now be transmitted to the delivering florist at any time of the day or night in writing, improving fulfillment accuracy and timeliness. For 15,000 florists throughout North America, it meant the end of the busy signal. In addition, order placement costs were reduced because many of the transmissions could be directed to the delivering florist at non-peak times when phone line usage charges were at their lowest point. Those florists not on the Mercury network receive their orders via telephone from FTD's Mercury Network headquarters in Chicago.

"That'll be 23 Fleurins, Please..."

The handling of an international wire order for flowers is relatively simple today, but once was a confusing and complicated transaction. As you might expect, one of the complexities was the currency exchange. Some years ago, FTD invented its own unit of currency, the "fleurin," to ease the way for consumers to send or receive flowers world-wide.

The value of the fleurin is pegged to the Swiss franc, except that it doesn't fluctuate every business day. Its value is fixed by FTD every six months and that value remains intact until the next adjustment.

L08499898C

When an international order is placed in the U.S., the value of the order is converted into units of fleurin at the prevailing rate and sent to the florist in the recipient's country in fleurin, If the fleurin value was currently set at 50 cents, for example, a $50 international order would become 100 fleurin. At the receiving end, then, the delivering florist would fill the order at the 100 fleurin level for that particular country.

Consumers don't need to know how all the "high finance" dealings work in the transaction between florists around the world. The important thing is that the order is fulfilled, the sender and recipient are happy, and the process is as simple as sending flowers to the next town.

Appendix 1: *What to Give for Anniversaries*

Year	Traditional	Modern
First	Paper	Clocks
Second	Cotton	China
Third	Leather	Crystal/Glas
Fourth	Fruit/Flowers	Appliances
Fifth	Wood	Silverware
Sixth	Candy	Wood
Seventh	Wood/Copper	Desk Sets
Eighth	Bronze/Pottery	Linens/lace
Ninth	Pottery/Willow	Leather
Tenth	Tin/Aluminum	Diamond Jewelry
Eleventh	Steel	Fashion Jewelry
Twelfth	Silk/Linen	Pearls

Year	Traditional	Modern
Thirteenth	Lace	Textiles/Furs
Fourteenth	Ivory	Gold Jewelry
Fifteenth	Crystal	Watches
Twentieth	China	Platinum
Twenty-fifth	Silver	Silver
Thirtieth	Pearl	Diamond
Thirty-fifth	Coral	Jade
Fortieth	Ruby	Ruby
Forty-fifth	Sapphire	Sapphire
Fiftieth	Gold	Gold
Fifty-fifth	Emerald	Emerald
Sixtieth	Diamond	Diamond

Appendix 2: Floral Industry Publications

FLORIST MAGAZINE
29200 Northwestern Highway
Southfield, MI 48307

FLORISTS' REVIEW
3641 SW Plass
Topeka, KS 66611-2588

FLOWERS &
12233 W. Olympic Blvd.
Los Angeles, CA 90064

FLORAL MANAGEMENT
1601 Duke Street
Alexandria, VA 22314

SUPER FLORAL MAGAZINE
10901 W. 84th Terrace
Lenexa, KS 66214

LINK
1600 King St.
Alexandria, VA

Appendix 3: Major Floral Industry Suppliers

FLORALIFE, INC.
120 Tower Drive
Burr Ridge, IL 60521

JH BUSINESS FORMS
4404 S. Creyts Rd.
Lansing, MI 48917
517-322-0770

A.L RANDALL
Lincolnshire, IL.
708-634-4300

DESIGNER DISPATCH
Plumsteadville, PA
215-766-2901

FLORALIFE, INC.
129 Tower Drive
Burr Ridge, IL
800-323-3689

KNUD NIELSEN CO.
Evergreen, AL
334-578-2900

LION RIBBON
Chester, NJ
800-551-LION

SMITHERS OASIS
919 Marvin Avenue
Kent, OH 44240
800-321-8286

SYNDICATE SALES
2025 N. Wabash Ave.
Kokomo, IN 46903
317-457-7277

FLOWERS INC. BALLOONS
Bogart, GA
800-241 2094

Appendix 4: Floral Industry Sources

The floral industry is populated with good, hard-working people who love to make their customers happy. If you would like to become a florist, contact some of your local floral retailers for assistance. some of them may even offer you a job, which would be the best kind of training for you.

If you would like information about the industry in general, these are some of the leading companies and associations you can contact:

SOCIETY OF AMERICAN FLORISTS
Peter Moran, Exec. VP/CEO
1601 Duke St.
Alexandria, VA. 22314
800-336-4743

SUPER FLORAL MAGAZINE
Carolyn Hathaway, Editor
10901 W. 84th Terrace
Lenexa, KS 66214

AMERICAN FLORAL SERVICES
Tom Butler, President
3737 N.W. 34th ST.
Oklahoma City, OK
800-456-7890

TELEFLORA, INC.

12233 W. Olympic Blvd.
Los Angeles, CA 90064
310-447-0229

HOLLAND FLOWER COUNCIL

212-980-2088
FAX 516-621-3923

COLOMBIA FLOWER COUNCIL

8725 NW 18 Terr Ste 106
Miami, FL 33172
305-477-9147

FTD ASSOCIATION

P.O. BOX 250455
Franklin, MI 48025
800-788-9000

HIXSON'S SCHOOL OF FLORAL DESIGN

14125 Detroit Ave.
Lakewood, OH 44107
216-521-9277

AMERICAN FLORAL ART SCHOOL

529 South Wabash
Chicago, IL 60605
312-922-9328

MCNES MARKETING AND ADVERTISING

Rick Nesbitt
3601 S.W. 29th St.
Suite 122
Topeka, KS 66614
785-271-0800

More About the Author...

On page 8, we shared a few esoteric musings about the author of this book, Harry Knitter. While we tried to be brief, we left out some key points about his background; for example, he has successfully completed several careers in his lifetime–as a marketing executive with Chrysler Marine, a vice-president with Ross Roy Advertising, Florists' Transworld Delivery Assn. (FTD), and The John Henry Company, all in Michigan. He won two American Management Association Gold Effie awards for marketing productivity and four top spot "quality and originality"
creative awards for campaigns in connection with Floraprint, Intl., an international horticultural organization.

Together with his wife, Nancy, he co-founded Kordene Publications in Okemos, Michigan and has published three books and written a fourth.

His books are titled: **HOLDING PATTERN: Airport Waiting Made Easy,** *a book that makes time fly when your plane doesn't;* **Why You Should Take Your Travel Agent to Lunch,** *the book to read before you book;* **101 Stupid Things Business Travelers Do to Sabotage Success,** *a book that demonstrates why it ain't smart to be stupid. He is also introducing two others titled,* **A Sweet Sampling of Floral Delights: For Anyone who Enjoys Getting, Giving, or Gazing at Flowers,** *and* **The Joys of Having Boys.**

He also plays the piano, has participated in the Detroit Tigers Fantasy Baseball Camp and shoots in the 90's on the golf course. For nine, of course, of course.

ORDER BLANK

Kordene Publications, P.O. BOX 911, Okemos, MI 48805-0911
or **call (888) 567-3363**

Please send me______copies of

"A Sweet Sampling of Floral Delights" by Harry Knitter

______@ $7.95 per copy, plus $3.00 per book for postage and handling.

My check, payable to Kordene, in the amount of $________ is enclosed.

Name____

Address____

City, State, Zip Code____________________________________

Michigan Residents add 6% State Sales Tax

ORDER BLANK

Kordene Publications, P.O. BOX 911, Okemos, MI 48805-0911
or **call (888) 567-3363**

Please send me_______copies of

"A Sweet Sampling of Floral Delights" by Harry Knitter

_______@ $7.95 per copy, plus $3.00 per book for postage and handling.

My check, payable to Kordene, in the amount of $________ is enclosed.

Name____

Address____

City, State, Zip Code_________________________________

Michigan Residents add 6% State Sales Tax